BELLS
THE FIRE DOG

First published in 2023

ISBN: 9798851943485

BELLS
THE FIRE DOG

Les Jones
with Steve Eggleston

Bells the Fire Dog is a spin off children's book with its background in the novel, *Twelve Doors,* also by Les Jones

Read more about *Twelve Doors* on its dedicated website, https://www.12doors.info.

1

Bells stretched out in her bed in the corner of the kitchen. Her muzzle rested on her paws as she snored gently, her ears and tail twitching as she slept. She was dreaming gentle, happy dreams where she was warm and safe, nuzzled up to her mother's soft furry belly with her brothers and sisters wriggling and snuffling next to her.

In the dream, Bells' belly was full of milk as her mother licked her clean and nudged her gently with her nose. Bells could hear the thump, thump, thump of her mother's heart lulling her to sleep. It was the best place to be in the world. It smelled of love and security.

But suddenly, the dream changed and Bells whimpered out loud. There was a strange horrible smell that burned her nostrils and stung her eyes. She couldn't breathe. She couldn't see a thing for all the swirling, thick, smoky stuff. And it was getting so hot. There was a frightening roaring noise and something huge, orange, and wild was dancing closer and closer. And it was still getting hotter and hotter and hotter…

Bells woke with a yelp. She was trembling and panting. She jumped out of her bed and paced around the kitchen her paws click clacking on the tiles. It was just another dream she told herself. Just a memory – of before. She wished her girl was here. Katie would know how to make her feel better. She would put her arms around Bells and hold her close. She would scratch behind Bells' ears and tell her everything was ok. And Bells would press herself close and sniff her girl's delicious smells of fresh grass and hidden treats. But Katie wasn't here and her other humans, Leah and Dave, were still out at work.

Bells went to her bowl and took a long drink of water. She shook herself hard to get rid of the nightmare, making her ears flap from side to side. Gradually she began to feel a bit better. Her heart was still heavy though. Because she knew the dream was real.

She flopped back down in her bed and reached around to lick the scar on her back, just behind her tail. Just like the horrible dreams, the scar was a reminder of everything Bells had lost that terrible day when a fire had burned down the shed she and her family were sleeping in. Bells remembered how her first human, Philip, had run in and out of the shed shouting and yelling. She remembered how he'd fought the orange flames, batting them back with his bare hands. And how, one by one, he'd carried Bells, her mother, and all the other puppies away from the fire and laid them out on the grass in the front garden. Bells remembered looking across at her mother and the other puppies lying so still on the grass. She wondered why they weren't moving. But then everything went black.

When Bells woke up she had found herself in a cage in a bright, white room. The light hurt her eyes. Her whole body hurt. All she wanted to do was sleep. When she woke up again she hurt a little bit less and her tummy rumbled with hunger. A kind doggie doctor in a white coat had placed a bowl of food in front of her. Bells gobbled it up quickly then looked up to see if there was a chance of any more. The kind doggie doctor was talking to another human on the other side of the room. "It's very sad," he was saying. "This puppy is so lucky to have survived the fire. Her mother and all the other puppies died."

Suddenly Bells wasn't hungry anymore. Instead, she had been filled with an awful sinking feeling as she realised she was now all alone in the world.

2

Bells stared out of the window at the grey sky. The rain was drumming down so hard it sounded like thousands of tiny pebbles being dropped from the sky.

Bells sighed and cocked her eye towards the kitchen clock. The big hand had to be pointing straight up before her girl came home from school, and it wasn't quite there yet. And until her girl came home, Bells couldn't get her ball back. Her favourite blue ball that she had left out in the garden. In the rain.

Bells loved that ball. On the day she left the doggy hospital to come and live with her new humans Leah, Dave, and Katie, the blue ball had been waiting for her in the car.

Bells remembered how frightened she had been on the journey from the hospital to the little house in Stockwood on Sea that was to become her new home. She had never been in a car before and the roar of the engine reminded her of the roar of the fire on that terrible, terrible day. But her new girl, Katie, had put her arms around Bells and held her close. She had shown her the blue ball and told her about all the games they would play together. She had stroked Bells' head and whispered calm words, so soon Bells relaxed and began to make sense of all the new and exciting smells that filled up the car.

Bells quickly settled into life in her new humans' house. They were so kind and gentle. They gave Bells a big soft bed to sleep on in the kitchen and every day they filled her bowl with delicious things to eat. And on Friday nights when they bought their tea from the fish and chip shop, they always brought back an extra piece of fish just for Bells.

Bells drooled at the thought of crunchy batter and soft, flaky fish. Was it Friday today? She hoped it was.

Suddenly there was a rattle at the front door. The sound of a key turning! Bells' ears pricked up and an excited bark bubbled up from her throat. She ran down the hallway, her tail wagging furiously. When the front door opened and Katie stepped inside, Bells burst into full-blown barks and flung herself at her girl's legs.

"Hey, girl," laughed Katie as she ruffled Bells' head. "I've missed you too!"

Bells' happy little yelps followed Katie down the hallway where she dumped her school bag. Bells kept her nose close to Katie's ankles as her girl opened the backdoor and ran out into the garden to rescue the blue ball.

"Is this what you've been waiting for? asked Katie.

Bells ran round and round in delighted circles. She didn't mind the fat drops of rain falling on her coat or the wet grass squelching between her paws. For the next few minutes, as Bells chased the blue ball around the garden, she forgot all about the frightening dream, the terrible fire, and the aching scar on her back. All that mattered was this wonderful world where she had her girl, her blue ball, and all the love she could ever wish for.

3

It was puppy training evening in the local village hall and Bells stood shyly by Katie's side watching all the other dogs being put through their paces. There were dogs of all shapes and sizes and so many different scents that Bells didn't know what part of the air to sniff next.

There was a yellow Labrador with gangly legs and huge paws, a tiny pug who wouldn't stop yapping, a Cockerpoo excitedly saying hello to everyone, a haughty Poodle looking down her nose at the busy room, and a French

Bulldog wearing a diamond encrusted collar.

Bells shuffled closer to Katie. "It's okay," said Katie. "I'm not going to leave you here on your own. I'll be with you every step of the way."

This was the first time Bells had been around so many other dogs. She wasn't sure how to behave. Should she say hello? Or should she wait for them to speak to her first? Would they like her? Or would they notice the scar on her back and want nothing to do with her?

"Hello!" came a voice from across the room. "My name's Frankie. What's yours?"

Bells looked up to see the Cockerpoo staring straight at her with a lopsided grin on his face. "I said, my name's Frankie. What's yours?" the Cockerpoo repeated.

"Erm, Bells. My name is Bells."

"Nice to meet you," said Frankie. He cocked his head to one side. "What are you?"

Bells frowned. She was confused. What am I? she thought. What did Frankie mean? "I'm…I'm a dog," said Bells eventually.

"Ha, ha, ha!" The Poodle burst into

laughter. "He means what breed are you? It's obvious you're a dog!"

Bells heard some of the other dogs sniggering. She lowered her head. How could she have been so stupid? She wished Katie would take her home, away from this place and these strange dogs.

"Yes," said Frankie. "What breed are you? You've definitely got Spaniel in you!"

Bells nodded. Why wouldn't they just leave her alone? "Cocker Spaniel," she murmured. "I'm a Cocker Spaniel."

"Ooh, you're a clever one, then," said Frankie. "You'll have no trouble with these puppy classes then. We'd better all watch out!"

Bells couldn't tell if Frankie was joking or not, but there was no time to decide as suddenly Katie was walking her to join in a line with all the other dogs and their humans.

The next hour passed in a blur and whir of voices, noise, and smells.

COME!

SIT!

STAY!

HEEL!

WAIT!

GIVE!

LEAVE IT!

There were tunnels to run through, and obstacles to run around and over. Bells soon learned that every time she did something right, Katie would reward her with a moment with her favourite blue ball.

"Good girl. Good girl." Katie ruffled Bells' head as Bells proudly held her blue ball in her mouth.

"Bonjour," said the French Bulldog who was sitting next to Bells. "My name is Fifi and j'adore le saucisson. Sausages, sausages! I only answer to sausages."

Bells watched as Fifi slurped down a chunk of sausage before setting off around the obstacle course again. "Long live ze sausage!" barked Fifi.

Sausages were all well and good, thought Bells. But nothing could beat her shiny, blue ball. She'd rather have that than all the sausages in the world.

Just then, the yappy pug, Cordelia, who

had been running around the room ignoring her human's calls, crashed into Bells. The blue ball fell from Bells' mouth and rolled across the floor coming to a stop directly in front of Frosty the Poodle.

Bells turned to grab it back. But she wasn't quick enough. Frosty placed his paw on top of the blue ball and with a wicked glint in his eye, said, "If you want your ball back, you're going to have to come and get it."

4

Bells lunged for the ball. But quick as a flash, Frosty batted it with his paw sending the ball flying across the other side of the room. Bells chased after it, desperate to get it back.

It was her ball. Her precious ball. Katie had given it to her. She couldn't lose it!

A horrible empty feeling filled Bells' tummy. The thought of losing her ball made her feel like she had when she lost her family. She didn't want to feel like that ever again. She was going to get her ball back no matter what.

She dashed across the hall, not caring who got in her way. She whizzed past Frankie, Cordelia and Fifi, whipping them and the other dogs into a state of excitement. Now they all wanted the blue ball and whoever was fastest was going to get it.

Suddenly, there was a complete uproar. Dogs barked and flew everywhere. Humans shouted.

LEAVE IT!

COME!

HEEL!

But none of the dogs took any notice. All eyes were on the blue ball. And Bells led the charge.

A table was tipped over, chairs went flying and even the trainer was knocked off her feet when Frankie crashed into her ankles.

It was pandemonium.

Bells was frantic. *Where's my ball? Where's my ball?* she panted as she ran around the hall. *Give me back my ball!*

Suddenly, a loud, shrill noise sliced through the air. All the dogs skidded to a halt and turned to see the trainer with a silver whistle in her mouth. "STOP!" the trainer shouted.

In the silence that followed, the humans rushed toward their dogs and grabbed hold of their collars. Bells felt Katie clip on her lead and gently pull her away. "Goodness me! What was that all about? That's no way to behave," said Katie crossly.

Bells' heart sank. She had so wanted to do well. She had wanted to show Katie what a good clever dog she was. And now, all because of Frosty the Poodle, everything was ruined. And where was her blue ball? Would she ever see it again? Was it lost forever like her mother and all her brothers and sisters? And what about Katie? And Leah and Dave? Would she lose them too? Would they want to keep her after all the chaos she had just caused?

The familiar empty feeling filled Bells' belly and chest. She felt hollow and terribly heavy all at the same time. She swallowed hard and whimpered to try and make the feeling go away.

Bells dragged her feet all the way home. She couldn't bring herself to look at Katie. As soon as they got back to the house, Bells ran into the kitchen and curled up in her bed making herself as small as possible.

The delicious smells of dinner being cooked wafted into her nostrils and the sounds of Katie, Leah, and Dave talking floated around in the air. Bells heard the tinkle of food being shaken into her dish, but she still didn't move. She wasn't even hungry. She was far too sad.

Just then she felt a hand on her head and fingers tickling her behind her ears just where she liked it. "Hey, Bells," said Katie. "Come on, girl. I'm not cross with you anymore. Really, I'm not."

Bells kept her head down. But her ears pricked up. Did Katie mean it? Was she really not cross anymore?

"It's okay to be sad," said Katie. "I know how much you loved your blue ball. And it wasn't your fault you lost it. You'll learn to love another ball again, I promise you will." Katie moved her hand to Bells' back and

25

pushed her fingers into her fur. "You know how much we love you, don't you?" she whispered.

Bells stirred and lifted her head. *It was all okay? Katie still loved her?* Bells slowly rolled over onto her back and whined softly. Katie laughed and began to tickle Bells' tummy. "And I forgive you," she said. "For causing such a fuss at puppy training classes. You'd better behave yourself next time we go!"

Bells licked Katie's hand. It tasted warm and salty and of home. Her tummy growled and she suddenly remembered the bowl of food waiting for her. With a happy little bark, she jumped to her feet and scampered over to her bowl with her tail wagging ten to the dozen.

5

The day after the disastrous puppy training class, Katie brought home a brand new ball for Bells. This new ball wasn't blue. It was a bright shiny red. Bells wasn't too sure of it at first. It didn't look like her old ball and it didn't smell like her old ball. She pushed it along the kitchen floor with her nose for a while, sniffing it suspiciously.

Katie laughed. "It's not going to bite you, Bells! C'mon, let's take it to the park and see how far I can throw it."

It was a beautiful, blustery day and as Bells trotted along beside Katic she lifted her nose to catch all the wonderful scents that danced in the wind. Then she put her nose to the ground to sniff the bottom of hedgerows and lamp posts trying to work out how many different dog scents she could pick up. The muddle of different smells told Bells it had been a busy morning. Twelve dogs had already walked this way. Two of them were ill, one of them was pregnant and another had eaten far too many chicken nuggets. A couple of cats had been this way too, and Bells looked around excitedly in case they were still nearby. Cats were good to chase. *Come on, come on, come and get me*, they always taunted, but Bells could never catch one. She couldn't climb trees for one thing, but that never stopped her from trying.

When they reached the park, Katie unclipped Bells' lead and with a yell of FETCH she threw the red ball as far as she could across the grass. Bells darted after it, her ears flapping madly and her tongue dangling from her mouth. She loved this game. She loved how her feet barely touched the ground as she sailed across the grass and how the air whizzed past her ears. But best of all, Bells loved how Katie made such a fuss of her when she brought the ball back and dropped it by her feet.

As Bells was running back to Katie for the umpteenth time she noticed something out of the corner of her eye that made her stop dead in her tracks. "What's the matter, Bells? Come on, girl. Bring the ball back," shouted Katie.

But Bells's eyes were fixed on the sight of a snowy white poodle trotting daintily over the grass on the other side of the park. Frosty!

A low growl rumbled at the back of Bells' throat as she held on extra tightly to her red ball.

Frosty and his human walked closer and closer. Bells noticed how well-clipped Frosty's fur was. And how clean he was! He was so clean he almost sparkled.

Frosty's human, a lady with a mean mouth and hard black eyes, looked down her pointy nose as she walked past Bells and Katie.

"Come on, Frosty," she shrilled. "Don't go near that dirty Spaniel. We don't want your nice clean coat to get spoiled, do we?"

Frosty glared at Bells as he trotted by, his eyes glinting at the red ball Bells still had clutched tightly in her mouth.

As they disappeared into the distance, Bells looked down at herself. Was she dirty? Yes, there was mud on her paws and belly and some grass stuck in her fur, but she and Katie had been having so much fun. And Bells knew Katie would rub her down with a nice soft towel when they got home. It didn't matter that she was dirty, did it?

"Come on," said Katie. "Time to go home."

As they walked back across the park, Katie bent down and hugged Bells. "Poor Frosty," she said. "Fancy not even being allowed to get his paws dirty. I do feel sorry for him. Don't you?"

Bells hadn't thought of it like that before. But Katie was right. It couldn't be much fun trying to stay clean all the time. No wonder Frosty had tried to take her ball if he wasn't allowed to play with one of his own.

Bells decide that at the next puppy training class she was going to try to be nice to Frosty. She might even let him sniff her new red ball.

6

Bells was true to her word and at the next puppy training class she made sure to be extra friendly to Frosty.

Frosty glared at Bells at first, as if to say, what's a scruffy dog like you doing bothering a glamorous dog like me?

But Bells took no notice. She circled Frosty, sniffing him all over, especially his bottom. Frosty growled and tried to nip Bells' ear. But Bells dodged out of the way and continued to sniff all along Frosty's tightly curled fur and under his high, tufty tail.

Frosty groaned. "You're not going to give up, are you?" he said.

"I just want us to be friends," said Bells. "Can we be friends? I'll let you play with my new red ball."

Frosty eyed the red ball that Katie was holding in her hand. "Do you think your human would let me?" he asked. Then he sighed. "I don't think my human would let me. She wouldn't want me to spoil my looks. I like being beautiful, but it's such hard work. Sometimes I wish I could just jump into a big muddy puddle."

"Then why don't you?" asked Bells.

"Because my human never lets me off the lead," said Frosty, sadly.

Bells thought for a moment. "I have an idea," she yapped excitedly. "What if you passed your puppy training classes with flying colours and came top of the class? If your human knew you were the best trained puppy ever, she might trust you enough to let you off the lead!"

"Do you think so?" asked Frosty.

"I know so!" said Bells.

For the next few weeks, at every puppy training class, Bells and Frosty worked harder than ever. They listened to every instruction and behaved perfectly.

They ran straight to their human when their name was called. They walked to heel, sat when they were told, and even learned to lie down and roll over. They didn't try to steal the other dogs' treats, they didn't bark or cause a fuss and when they needed the toilet they whined at their human to let them know they needed to be taken outside – unlike some of the other puppies who were still having little accidents on the floor.

The puppy trainer was so impressed with Bells and Frosty that at the end of the very last class, she pinned bright purple BEST PUPPY rosettes on their collars.

Bells' fluffy chest puffed up with pride. "Oh, well done," exclaimed Katie, bending down to give Bells a huge hug. "I always knew you were the best!"

Frosty looked delighted with himself too. His human even managed to pat him on his head, being careful not to ruffle his fur too much.

"See you at the park," Bells barked as she followed Katie outside.

"I hope so," Frosty barked back. "I really hope so."

A few days later, during a drizzly afternoon walk in the park, Bells saw a white shape in the distance zig-zagging wildly across the grass.

"Frosty!" a human voice yelled. "Come! Come here now!"

Bells grinned to herself. Good old Frosty. There he was having the time of his life, running with the wind through puddles and mud, his white fur splattered and bedraggled, his eyes sparkling with the joy of freedom.

The weeks and the months passed by and Bells grew bigger and stronger. Her fur shone, her legs grew to match her feet, and her tail wagged non-stop. She remembered every single lesson from the puppy training classes and loved to make Katie, Leah and Dave proud.

She often saw Frosty at the park and would run up to him to say hello. Sadly for Frosty, his human wouldn't let him off the lead again. "But I don't mind," Frosty told Bells. "That first time, when she let me off thinking

I would stay by her side, but I ran off and rolled in all the muddy puddles, is my best memory and I wouldn't change it for the world, even though I had to spend hours at the poodle parlour afterwards."

"I'm sorry," said Bells with a shudder. "That must have been awful."

"Not really," said Frosty. "It's not as bad as you think. The humans at the parlour make me look so pretty. And I love being pretty." He tossed his head. "I've already won three Prettiest Dog in the Show trophies, and one day I'm going to win the big one!"

"What's that?" asked Bells.

"Crufts of course," said Frosty. "The biggest and best dog show in the entire world! And when I do, I'll be SO famous, just you wait and see!"

With that, Frosty trotted off beside his human, his pom-pom tail flicking prettily from side to side. Bells was glad that Frosty was happy with his lot and even gladder that Katie had never taken *her* to a poodle parlour.

Even though the scar on her back reminded Bells every day of the fire that killed her mother and brothers and sisters, her life now was perfect just as it was. She didn't want a thing about it to change.

8

Bells didn't know it yet, but change was coming. A huge change, and it was just around the corner.

One morning, just after Katie had left for school, Leah came into the kitchen carrying Bells' lead. Bells ran around in little circles. She wagged her tail and gave a couple of excited yelps as Leah clipped on her lead.

"And so you should be excited," laughed Leah. "You're coming to work with me today! What do you think of that?"

Work? thought Bells. Work? It sounded

like walk. Is that what Leah meant? A walk with her instead of Katie? But instead of going down the path and out of the front gate, Leah led Bells to the car and lifted her onto the back seat. Bells lay down quietly, her muzzle on her paws and her heart beating fast. What was this? Where was Leah taking her? She hoped it wasn't to the poodle parlour or the doggie doctor.

The car engine roared to life and Bells' heart beat even faster. "You know I work at the fire station, don't you Bells?" said Leah as she drove the car. "Well, I think you're big enough and clever enough to come with me now. You're going to be the fire station mascot. Isn't that exciting?"

Mascot? Mascot? Bells didn't know what that word meant. But there was one word she did know the meaning of and it sent shivers of fear right through her body from her nose to the tip of her tail.

FIRE! FIRE! FIRE!

That word meant hot and smoke and burning and hurt. It meant pain and terror and sadness. It meant roaring flames taking her mother and brothers and sisters away. Why would Leah be taking her somewhere where there was fire?

Bells whimpered softly and when Leah finally stopped the car, Bells refused to get out. "Come on, silly," said Leah. "What's the matter? There are lots of people here who want to meet you."

Bells sniffed the air. She couldn't smell anything dangerous, so very slowly, and keeping her belly close to the ground, she jumped out of the car and followed Leah through a wide door and into a large building.

Inside the building were two enormous red trucks with long ladders on the top. And standing around the trucks chatting were eleven other humans. "Hello, everyone," said Leah. "Come and meet Bells."

Bells pressed herself against Leah's leg as one by one the humans, some men, and some women, came over to greet her.

"Hello, girl. Come to join us have you?"

"Aren't you gorgeous, hey?"

"Good girl. Good girl."

Finally, when all the humans had finished

patting her head and had wandered away, Bells suddenly caught the unmistakable scent of CAT!

She whipped her head around, and there, in the corner of the room, casually licking its paws was a black cat! Bells' hackles rose and a low growl escaped from her throat. But before she had time to do anything, the cat looked up and stared Bells straight in the eye.

"Don't even think about chasing me," it said. "You'll never catch me. And besides, I live here, and the humans at this fire station wouldn't let you chase me."

FIRE! There was that word again. Bells began to tremble. "Fire?" she said. "Fire? Where's the fire? Fire is bad."

The cat laughed. "No, silly," it said. "There's no fire here. This is the fire station. See all those humans? They are firefighters. They help to put out fires. They put on special uniforms and drive the big red trucks to wherever there is a fire and they help to put it out and save lives. Didn't you know that?"

Bells shook her head.

"They can't always save lives though,"

said the cat. "They couldn't save your mother and brothers and sisters, even though they tried their very best."

Bells was shocked. "How did you know about my family?" she said.

The cat walked over to Bells and sat beside her. "Your old home, where you lived with your first human isn't too far from here. I was out on one of my daily prowls when the fire started. I saw what happened to your family and I knew that you'd been saved and had gone to live with Leah. I hoped I'd meet you one day. And here you are."

"You saw the fire?" said Bells in astonishment. She looked around at all the humans in the fire station. "But why couldn't these...these...firefighters put it out?"

The cat sighed. "Sometimes a fire is just too fierce and too fast. They tried their hardest to put it out though. I saw them. They tried their very best."

Bells sighed and flopped down on her belly. The cat lay down beside her. "You were very lucky," it said. "You survived and now you have a new home and humans who love you."

Bells was quiet for a moment. The cat was right. She was lucky. She was lucky to be alive. She was lucky to have Katie and Leah and Dave. And she was lucky to be in this place now, where these humans, these firefighters, did this amazing thing.

"Anyway," said the cat. "My name is Tom. Nice to meet you."

Bells slowly got used to life at the fire station. Whenever Leah went to work there, Bells went too. All the firefighters were so friendly and were always happy to see her.

Sometimes she would sit by the side of the big red fire engines as some of the crew washed them down with soapy water and then polished them until Bells could see her reflection in the red paint.

Some days the crew sat at a table playing cards and drinking tea. There were always packets of biscuits and crisps and if Bells sat under the table, one of the crew would always sneak her a tasty nibble or two.

The best days were when children from nearby schools came to visit. The firefighters showed them the fire engines with their giant hoses and ladders and explained how everything worked. The children were allowed to climb onto the fire engines to see everything up close. Bells loved listening to all their excited voices and barked happily when they rang the bell.

The firefighters taught the children all about the dangers of fire, and how it could quickly spread and hurt people and destroy homes. They showed the children a special Fire Triangle. One side of the triangle was red with the word HEAT. Another side was blue with the word OXYGEN, and the third side was brown with the word FUEL. The firefighter explained to the children that fire was a chemical reaction and needed all three of these things – HEAT, OXYGEN, and FUEL – to start and continue to burn.

Bells always sat quietly and listened to the firefighters warning the children not to ever play with matches and lighters. They taught the children about smoke alarms and how they keep homes safe from fire. They also talked about what to do in an emergency if there was a fire and how to call 999.

After all the talking was finished and all the questions were asked, the children would crowd around Bells taking turns to stroke her and tickle her behind the ears.

The worst days were when the fire crew left the station dressed in their black uniforms and bright yellow helmets and came back from a SHOUT with sadness spread across their faces. On those occasions, they slumped in their chairs and a heavy silence filled the fire station. Bells could smell the leftover scent of smoke and danger on their clothes and knew, without anyone saying a word, that they had seen some horrible things.

Luckily, those sorts of days were few and far between. Most of the time, when the crew came back from fighting a fire, they had smiles on their faces and only good stories to tell.

Bells got used to seeing the crew dressed

in their black uniforms and shiny yellow helmets. Only Leah wore a different helmet. Hers was white with black stripes. Tom the cat told Bells that was because Leah was an officer – the leader of the pack.

Even when the firefighters' faces were hidden away behind strange masks and they were carrying tanks of air on their backs, Bells knew exactly who was who.

Bells loved to watch the firefighters practising how to use the fire hose. They called it a drill and they had to do one every Tuesday evening at 6 o'clock. The fire hose was rolled up into a big circle. It was really heavy, and the crew had to practice how to lift it in exactly the right way and carry it on their shoulders. They had to practice how to connect the hose to the water pump and how to unroll it. And most importantly, they had to practice how to hold the hose when water came blasting out of it to help put out a fire.

There was a ladder drill at the same time too, where all the crew had to listen to their pack leader shouting commands. They had to practice making the ladder longer, carrying it to where it was needed, and putting it in just the right place.

Bells listened and learned and soon she knew just as much as all the humans. Even though she couldn't carry the ladder or unroll the hose herself, she knew just how things should be done and would bark if any of the crew members were too slow or got it wrong.

Tom the cat often sat next to Bells and watched the drills too, when he wasn't off prowling around the neighbourhood. The crew thought it was funny that Bells and Tom had become firm friends. "Look at those two," they would say. "Thick as thieves. Never seen anything like it. They should be fighting like…like cat and dog!!"

Bells didn't mind that the crew found her friendship with Tom funny. What did it matter that he was a cat and she was a dog? Tom was kind. He understood what Bells had lost when her family died. He remembered Bells' mother too and her gentle human Philip. He would tell Bells stories about seeing her mother and Philip out on their daily walks. It made Bells feel better to know her mother had been loved by a caring human.

The weeks and months passed by and soon Bells' puppy days were behind her as she grew into a fine young dog. A hot summer turned into a cold winter and soon it was the time of year when humans brought a tree into their house and hung it with coloured lights. The fire station had its own tree too, and the sharp, pine scent of it tickled Bells' nose.

Lots of humans from Stockwood on Sea were invited to the fire station for something called a Christmas fete. There were tables laid out with cakes and cups and plates. There were games to play and prizes to win. There was laughter and singing and a man dressed in red with a long white beard brought presents for the children.

Bells wandered through the crowd snuffling up tasty crumbs that had been dropped on the ground and stopping every second or so for a stroke or a pat on her head. It seemed as though the whole of Stockwood on Sea knew who she was now.

Katie told her she was the most famous

dog in town and had even made Bells her own special page on her computer. It was called Facebook, Katie explained, and it was full of photos of Bells and of all the things she got up to at the fire station. There were even some photos of Tom the cat.

No matter what a day at the fire station brought, Bells always went home to Katie. As time went on, the scar above her tail seemed to ache less and less, and the ache in her heart faded too.

10

It was the middle of the night and all was quiet in the little house in Stockwood on Sea. Leah and Dave were asleep in their bedroom upstairs and Katie was asleep in hers.

Bells was curled up snugly in her bed in the kitchen dreaming of chasing the squirrels she sometimes saw in the park. She whimpered softly and her legs paddled as she darted after giant bushy tails.

Suddenly, her nose and ears began to twitch and she slowly opened her eyes. What was that strange smell? And what was that crackling, sizzling noise? Bells jumped to her feet, the giant squirrels of her dream forgotten. Her nose and ears twitched faster as she padded from the kitchen into the living room. She could smell danger. It was close by. The smell grew stronger and the noise grew louder.

Then Bells saw it. A curling wisp of smoke and bright orange sparks came from behind the Christmas tree which was still twinkling with coloured lights.

Bells stiffened.

Fire!

A ripple of fear ran down her back.

As she watched, more curls of smoke appeared and the orange sparks burst into angry, flickering flames.

She had to warn them! She had to warn Leah and Dave and Katie!

Bells ran out to the hallway and stood at the bottom of the stairs. BARK! BARK! BARK! She stopped and listened. No sound of movement came from upstairs. They hadn't heard her! She barked louder. Still nothing.

Bells cocked her head and stared at the stairs. She wasn't usually allowed up there. That was her humans' space. She glanced back at the living room. But the danger – the fire – was growing bigger. All Bells' senses were on red alert. She knew she had to act now.

Bells bounded up the stairs and pushed open the door to Leah and Dave's bedroom with her nose. Bark! Bark! Bark!

She grabbed hold of their duvet with her teeth and pulled hard until it slid off the bed.

"What…what? What's going on?" Dave's voice mumbled.

"What's the matter? What is it?" said Leah's sleepy voice.

BARK! BARK! BARK! Bells ran towards the bedroom door and then back to Dave and Leah. BARK! BARK! BARK! She ran to the door again.

"I think she wants us to follow her," said Dave. "Okay, girl, it's okay, we're coming."

"What's happening?" said Katie stumbling into the room. "What's all the noise about?"

"We don't know," said Dave. "But something has spooked Bells and she wants us to go with her."

Bells led the way, barking over her shoulder, as Leah, Dave, and Katie followed her to the top of the stairs.

"Okay, we're coming, we're coming. It's alright, girl," said Dave, as they all ran down the stairs.

"Wait!" said Dave, as they all gathered in the hallway. "I can smell burning!" He poked his nose into the living room, then shouted, "Right, everyone! Outside! Get into the garden, now! I'll call 999! Looks like the Christmas tree lights have caught fire! We forgot to unplug them before we went to bed!"

Bells followed Dave, Leah, and Katie into the garden where they all stood shivering in their pyjamas. A few minutes later the wail of sirens sliced through the cold night air.

Bells stood by Katie's side and watched as her friends from the fire station jumped into action. Leah's 2nd in command, John Turnbull was leading the crew and before long, the fire was extinguished. Because Bells had sounded the warning so early, the only damage was a scorched Christmas tree and a melted plug.

"You had a very lucky escape," said John. He knelt to stroke Bells. "If it hadn't been for this clever lady waking you up in time, things might have turned out very differently indeed."

Dave and Leah nodded solemnly.

"Oh, Bells," said Katie as she put her arms around Bells' neck and held her close. "You saved our lives! You really are one special dog!"

11

A few weeks after the Christmas tree fire, Leah and Dave sat at the kitchen table chatting. Bells lay on the floor beside them gnawing on a tasty dog chew.

"I think she'd be perfect," Leah said. "She's so intelligent and willing to learn and look how she warned us about the fire."

"But it would mean her moving to London. It would mean her leaving us," said Dave.

"I know," said Leah, sadly. "But the fire service needs dogs like Bells, and the selection process starts in two weeks."

Bells cocked her ear at the mention of her name. *London? Leaving? What were Leah and Dave saying?*

She didn't have to wait long to find out.

When Katie came home from school later that day, Bells heard Leah and Dave talking again about London and fire investigation dogs and a selection process. *What did it all mean and why was Katie so sad?*

When Katie knelt to clip on Bells' lead ready for her evening walk, her eyes were wet. Bells whimpered and pressed her face close to Katie's to lick away the salty tears. Katie laughed half-heartedly. "Oh Bells, you know something's up, don't you? But it's nothing bad. I promise."

They walked their usual route along rain-soaked streets and under the blurry yellow glow of street lights. Katie didn't chatter on like she usually did and this worried Bells so much that she didn't even put her nose to the ground to sniff all the interesting smells. Instead, she trailed along behind Katie whining softly.

Finally, just when Bells couldn't bear the

sad silence any longer, Katie began to talk. "You know how much we love you, don't you Bells?" she said, sniffing back her tears. "But the thing is, you're too smart to live with us forever."

What did she mean? thought Bells. *Too smart?*

"I wish you *could* stay with us forever," Katie continued. "But that would be a waste of your talents."

As they slowly walked through the evening drizzle, Katie told Bells all about fire investigation dogs and how, with their amazing sense of smell, they were able to sniff out all the things that started a fire, such as petrol, paint, oil or gas. This helped the firefighters to learn how a fire started and how to stop it from happening again. Fire dogs also helped to find people trapped in buildings that were on fire and to save lives. "It's a very important job," Katie explained. "And we think you would be perfect for it."

She told Bells how she would travel to a big, noisy city called London. She would be put through lots of tests before being chosen to be part of the fire dog team. She would make loads of new friends and best of all she would have a new human called Poppy. Poppy was a firefighter like Leah, and she would help Bells with her training. "She'll be your handler," Katie explained. "And you'll be her first dog too. So you can help each other to learn the ropes."

Katie stopped and knelt down to hug Bells. "And we'll come and visit you as often as we can," she promised. "You're going to make us so proud. I just know you are."

Alone in her bed that night, Bells found it hard to settle. She felt sad, afraid, and excited all at the same time. She didn't want to leave Leah and Dave and Katie. They were her humans. She trusted and loved them, and couldn't imagine living with anyone else. She didn't want to leave all her friends at Stockwood on Sea fire station either. Especially not Tom the cat. But maybe if she went to this place called London and trained to be a fire dog, she could learn how to save people and animals from fires. And if she could stop just one puppy from losing its family in a fire as she had, that would be a good thing, wouldn't it?

12

The sky was a bright blue and the air was crispy cold on the morning Bells left the little house in Stockwood on Sea. Dave loaded her bed and toys into his car, including her treasured red ball, before everyone else jumped in too.

Bells sat next to Katie in the back of the car, her heart beating fast at the thought of all the strange new things that lay ahead. Katie rested her hand on Bells' head, gently stroking behind her ears.

Dave stopped the car at the fire station first

and all the crew came out to say goodbye.

"Good luck."

"You'll be amazing."

"We'll miss you!"

Bells spotted Tom the cat sitting on a nearby wall.

"Uff! Uff!" Bells woofed, a sad feeling twisting her heart.

Tom looked across at Bells and nodded knowingly. "It was good being your friend," he purred. "I don't like dogs as a rule, but I was happy to make an exception for you. Just remember, everyone has a place and you're going where you're meant to be."

He jumped off the wall and sauntered off with his tail in the air. Then he stopped and looked back one last time. "And just so you know. You would never have caught me. Even if you'd tried to chase me!"

The journey to London seemed to last forever. Bells stared out of the car window as rooftops, trees and clouds whizzed past. A couple of times Bells nodded off listening to the voices singing out of the radio box in the car. When she woke up, the sky outside seemed smaller. It was crowded with different sizes and shapes of rooftops and giant buildings that reached into the clouds. There was a constant hum of noise too. The roar of car engines and the blare of honking horns filled the car.

Was this busy, noisy place London?

As if she'd heard her thoughts, Katie bent down and whispered in Bells' ear. "We're here, girl. We're almost in Croydon. We're almost at your new home."

Dave drove the car around a few more bends and corners until it finally slowed to a stop. Bells twisted around to peer out the back window and saw a long street lined with yellow brick houses, the doors all painted in bright colours.

"That one's your new home," said Katie pointing to a house with a door painted the same shade of red as Bells' favourite ball.

As Bells stared at the red door it suddenly opened and a human with a huge smile on her face came running towards the car. Bells squashed herself against Katie. She felt shy and not sure she wanted to meet this bouncy new human. "It's okay," said Katie. "Come on, let's go and say hello to Poppy."

Bells hopped out of the car after Katie and stood quietly as the humans greeted each other. When they had all finished talking, the new human Poppy, bent down and held her hand out to Bells.

Bells sniffed Poppy's hand cautiously. It smelt good. It smelt of kindness and happiness and safety. Bells' tail began to wag.

"I think she likes you," laughed Katie.

"Well, I certainly like her!" said Poppy. She ruffled Bells' head. "We're going to be the best of friends, aren't we? I can just tell."

Poppy led everyone into her house where they all stood around for a while drinking tea and chatting. Bells lay on the floor next to Katie as the voices drifted over her head. This new house didn't smell dangerous or scary. It felt friendly and warm like one of Katie's hugs.

When the humans had finished talking and drinking, Dave went out to the car to fetch Bells' bed and toys. Then all too soon it was time to say goodbye. Dave and Leah ruffled Bells' fur one last time and Katie wrapped her arms around Bells' neck and buried her face in her fur. "I love you," she whispered. "And I'm going to miss you like mad."

As they walked out of the front door, Bells ran to the window and stood on her hind legs to see out. She watched as Dave, Leah and Katie climbed into their car and closed the doors. Katie's face peered out at her and a small howl escaped from Bells' throat. She watched as the car drove down the street and disappeared around a corner. She stayed at the window for a long time, staring at the empty space left behind.

13

The first night at Poppy's house was so strange that Bells couldn't stop howling. She wanted her girl. She missed Katie so much that it hurt. She missed the familiar scents and noises of the little house in Stockwood on Sea. And even though her new human Poppy stroked her gently and tried to calm her with soothing words, Bells felt utterly alone for the second time in her life.

When she finally fell asleep, exhausted from all her howling, Bells dreamt she was in the park with Katie. Her girl threw the red ball and Bells ran and ran and ran, her paws spinning over the grass. She grabbed the ball in her mouth and turned to run back to her girl. But no matter how fast she ran, Katie got further and further away. Bells couldn't catch her, no matter how hard she tried. She was losing her girl and a howl of grief rose from her chest and woke her up.

A pair of arms reached out for her in the darkness. The arms held her close and rocked her gently until she finally fell asleep again.

When Bells woke up the next morning, the sun was streaming through the window and her new human, Poppy, was lying on the floor next to her, still fast asleep.

After a few days, Bells stopped running to the window every few minutes, and instead began to sit by Poppy's feet when she was working at her desk or relaxing in her chair in the evenings. She grew used to the new smells in the house and when Poppy took her out for walks in this new neighbourhood called Croydon, there was so much to see, sniff and explore that Bells sometimes forgot to miss Katie.

But every night when Bells fell asleep in her bed, Katie was always there in her thoughts and deep in her heart.

One morning, just after Bells had finished her breakfast, Poppy announced that the big day had arrived. She was taking Bells to see the doggie doctor, a kind human called Steven, to check she was in tip top condition, then they were off to join the first of the special fire dog training classes.

Bells knew this day was coming. It was the reason she'd moved to London after all. She didn't mind the thought of a visit to the doggie doctor. She had been to doggie doctors before so they could treat the burn scar behind her tail, and she knew they were all kind humans who only wanted to help animals. But the thought of the other place – the dog training classes – made her tummy churn uncomfortably.

Bells was right about Steven the doggie doctor. He had sparkling eyes that crinkled at the corners, warm, gentle hands and a voice that made Bells want to jump into his lap and lick his face.

Bells stood on a metal table as Steven examined her all over, noting how bright and alert she was, how her coat and eyes shone with health and how her teeth, ears and eyes were all perfectly healthy too.

"Clean bill of health," he said to Poppy. "Now just one more thing to do."

Steven the doggie doctor lifted Bells' leg and carefully wiped it with a piece of wet cloth. "This will sting a bit," he said as he pushed a long, shiny needle into Bells' leg. Bells trusted Steven so she sat perfectly still and tried not to whimper. "Good girl," said the doggie doctor. "There, all finished."

After Bells had been lifted down from the table, Steven the doggie doctor fished around in his pockets and brought out a small meaty treat. Bells gobbled it up gratefully. It tasted so delicious that she immediately forgot all about the little pain in her leg where the needle had been.

Bells jumped happily into the back of Poppy's car. She was glad the visit to the doggie doctor was over. She licked her lips, trying to taste the last traces of the meaty treat. It was only when the car began to move that Bells remembered Poppy was taking her somewhere else too.

And that somewhere else was far scarier than any visit to the doggie doctor or any needle could ever be.

14

The large room was full of dogs of all sizes and colours and breeds. There was a Dalmatian, a German shepherd, a Labrador Retriever, a Border Collie and a Pointer – almost too many for Bells to count. She stayed close to Poppy's side as the human in charge called for quiet and began to shout out every dog's name.

Turnout!

Bells!

Aqua!

Smoky!

Squirt!

Scout!

Shout!

Buddy!

Ralph!

Marley!

Cooper!

Teddy!

All the dogs stood to attention, their muzzles forward and their eyes fixed on the human in charge. This wasn't like puppy training classes, this was serious stuff.

There was one dog in the room who was larger than all the rest. The brown fur around his muzzle was speckled white, there was a deep scar across his nose and his eyes were the wisest Bells had ever seen. When the human in charge stopped speaking, this tough-looking, tattered around the edges dog stepped forward.

"My name is Turnout," he barked. "And for the next six weeks, I will be in charge of you all. I have been a fire dog for many years. I have seen many things. Some good and some bad. I have saved many lives..." he bowed his head... "and I have lost some lives." There was silence for a moment. The other dogs in the room looked around at each other. Some whispered under their breath.

Was this the legendary Turnout? The dog who attended the horrific tower block fire a few years ago? The dog who put his own life in grave danger over and over again when he ran in and out of that blazing building trying to bring people out alive?

The dogs stared at Turnout in wonder. It was hard to believe that one dog could be so brave.

"Now listen, you mangy mutts" barked Turnout. "The next few weeks are going to be tough going for you. You are going to have to work harder than you have ever done in your life. I am going to teach you everything I know. But at the end of six weeks, not all of you will have made it. But those of you that do, will be the best trained fire dogs the service has to offer." He paused and looked sternly at each dog in turn. "Some of you may get injured in the line of duty, and some of you may even die. But what you must all remember is that saving lives is the most important thing any of us can do."

There was a long silence as each dog thought about what Turnout had just said.

"Do you think you'll make it?" the Dalmatian sitting next to Bells suddenly whispered. "I most certainly will. We Dalmatians have a long history of working for the fire service. In America, hundreds of years ago, our breed was chosen to work as carriage dogs. We could run great distances and our white coats with black spots made us easy to see. My American ancestors would run ahead of the horse-drawn carriages that carried all the fire equipment, bravely clearing the way with their barking." The Dalmatian tossed his head with pride. "We Dalmatians were the very first fire alarm sirens."

Bells wasn't quite sure what to say. "Well...I'm... sure you'll make it through then."

"No doubt about it," said the Dalmatian. "And I'm Cooper by the way. I'm sure you'll hear my name a lot."

Meet Bells, 2 years old

Meet Turnout

15

Turnout was as good as his word. In the days that followed, Bells worked harder than she had ever thought possible.

Every day, she and all the other dogs were given several containers to sniff. Inside the containers were fire starters – tiny drops of gas, oil and petrol that the humans called accelerants.

Each fire starter had its own scent which only a well-trained dog nose could smell. Turnout and his human handler would hide small amounts of fire starters all around the building or outside and Bells and the other dogs would be sent off to find them. First, the fire starters were hidden in one room, then in several rooms, then across different floors of a building. But most challenging of all was when the fire starters were hidden in letter boxes and under stairs and hard to get at places. Luckily, Bells managed to sniff out each and every one. But sadly, Smoky the Pointer, Scout the Labrador, Ralph the Spaniel, and Aqua the Border collie all failed the first test and were sent home with their tails between their legs.

As a reward for sniffing out the fire starters, each dog was given a reward. Bells' reward was always her red ball, but some of the other dogs liked a meaty treat or a tiny piece of sausage.

Every time Bells caught the scent of sausage in the air she remembered her days at puppy training classes and she wondered what all the dogs she'd met there were doing now. She wondered especially about Frosty the Poodle. Was he still as pretty as a picture and had his dream of winning Crufts ever come true?

She wished they could all see her now, expertly sniffing out fire starters. Each time Bells found the correct fire starter, she was given her red ball as a reward. And the more fire starters she found, the more time she was allowed to play with her ball. Sometimes it was hard for Bells to find the right scent among all the other smells floating around in the air. She worried about making a mistake. But the thought of her red ball helped her to focus and before long she could hunt out every single fire starter in double quick time.

"That's good," said Turnout. "You caught on fast. But it's only half the job. Now you must learn about what to do after you've found the fire starter. This is the most important part."

But Bells was tired. Her head was full of all the new things she'd learned and she didn't think there was room for any more stuff. All she wanted was a bowl of food and her nice, soft bed.

"Can't I just go home now?" said Bells. "I've found all the fire starters."

"Home?" growled Turnout. "Home? Do you think when there's a fire raging, burning down someone's house, we just go home when we're tired? Do you think when there's a small human trapped inside a burning building that we just go home because we've had enough?" Turnout bared his teeth. "With that attitude, you're NEVER going to make it as a fire dog. I should grant your wish and send you home NOW. Never to come back!!"

Bells shrank back and flattened her ears. She hadn't meant to make Turnout angry. She really hadn't. And she did want to make it through the fire dog training. She wanted to become a proper fire dog and help the firefighters in their brave work. She thought about her mother and her brothers and sisters and felt ashamed she had given up so easily.

"I'm sorry," she said. "Please let me stay. I promise from now on I'll do everything you say. Just please let me stay."

Turnout's eyes softened. "It would be a shame to lose a young dog with your ability. So yes, just this once, I'll forget about your whining. But don't let me down again, do you hear?"

"I won't, I won't," yapped Bells. "Thank you, thank you."

For the rest of the day and all the days that followed, Bells thought of nothing else but her training. She listened carefully as Turnout told her and the other dogs all about Alerts.

"As soon as you sniff out and find a fire starter you have to let your human handler know. You have to get their attention. This is called an Alert. You need to wag your tail in excitement and run around in circles. Then your human will know you have found the fire starter and you can lead them to it. And every time you do this you will get your reward."

When Bells held her red ball in her mouth she always remembered Katie and Stockwood-on-Sea and all the friends she had left behind to do this important thing. She wanted to prove to them all that she could do it. That she could become a real-life fire dog. And maybe, one day, she might end up as brave and heroic as Turnout.

16

As the weeks passed by and the days gradually grew longer and warmer, Bells grew even taller and stronger. When she wasn't hard at work training, she spent her time with her handler, Poppy.

She was Poppy's dog now, and although Katie often came to her in her dreams, the memory of the little house in Stockwood on Sea began to fade, like the remembered warmth of the sun on a hot day. And no matter how hard she tried to catch it, the scent of Katie was now lost to Bells.

Poppy was her human and on the weekends, Bells loved nothing better than to walk the streets of London by Poppy's side and to breathe in all the wonderful, exciting new sounds and smells that crowded the air.

The pavements were littered with the scents of strange dogs, foxes, cats and the footprints of thousands of humans. Bells was shocked to see dozens of street dogs slinking around corners, searching through bins for scraps and sleeping in shop doorways. She felt sad for them and wondered how they managed to survive without a human to look after them. Some of them looked so bedraggled and hungry that Bells wished she could take them home with her.

Then there were the other types of dogs. Tiny dogs being pushed around in human baby buggies, or being carried in bags on their humans' backs. Dogs dressed in coats and jumpers, some with ribbons in their hair and some with fancy leads and collars. Were they some strange breed that was half human, half dog? Bells wasn't sure and she stared at them curiously as she passed them in the street.

One Saturday afternoon, when Bells and Poppy were walking along the banks of the River Thames watching the brightly coloured boats sailing along, the sound of a siren suddenly ripped through the air. It didn't sound like the wail of a fire engine, it was faster somehow, with a different rhythm.

As Bells turned her head to see where the noise was coming from, a man dashed by, running for all he was worth. The siren came closer and closer and then a police van appeared from around the corner and skidded to a stop. A couple of policemen jumped from the van followed by two of the fiercest looking dogs Bells had ever seen. The dogs tore after the running man with the policemen close on their heels.

The man stood no chance. Within seconds the dogs had caught up with him and pushed him to the ground. They gripped on to his clothes with their sharp teeth as their warning growls filled the air.

Poppy and Bells watched as the two policemen ran over and called the dogs off.

They hoisted the man to his feet and clamped a pair of handcuffs to his wrists.

"He must have done something pretty bad," said Poppy. "For the police dogs to have chased him like that."

Police dogs! Bells stared at them in awe as they strutted back to the police van. Their muscles rippled under their fur and their yellow eyes glinted without a trace of fear. These were dogs who demanded respect and Bells bowed her head as they walked passed, resisting the urge to run over and sniff their bottoms.

Later on that same day, Poppy took Bells to Buckingham Palace. They stood in front of the huge metal gates as Poppy told Bells all about the King who lived inside. The guards who stood at the gates in their smart red uniforms had strange furry creatures sitting on their heads. Bells barked and barked at them until Poppy told her they were bearskin helmets and not real creatures at all.

They finished the day off with a run around Hyde Park. It was the biggest park Bells had ever seen with an enormous pond full of swans and friendly ducks who quacked hello as Bells and Poppy strolled by.

That night, as Bells snuggled down in her bed, she felt the happiest she had ever been. She had her human, Poppy, a warm place to sleep every night, plenty of delicious food to eat, and her precious red ball.

If she could just get through the last few days of training and become an official fire dog that would be the gravy on the sausage!

17

Bells!
    Squirt!
Shout!
Marley!
Cooper!
Teddy!
Buddy!

Every dog that had made it through to the end of training stood to attention as Turnout barked out their names. They were now officially Fire Dogs. Bells lifted her chin proudly as the Fire Chief pinned a badge to her collar.

"Congratulations, mutts!" barked Turnout. "Now you can sniff out over thirty different fire starters which humans can't detect with their own noses. And if a fire is caused deliberately, you will know how to find the exact place where it started. And most importantly, you know how to lead your handler to that place."

Turnout paused and eyed each dog in turn. "You will also be called upon to search burning buildings for anybody trapped inside. It is a dangerous job and you will need to use all your skills."

Turnout placed his paw on the gleaming badge pinned to his collar. "Now get out there and save some lives!"

"Uff! Uff! This is the best day of my life," said Cooper the Dalmatian as he lifted his chin to receive his badge too. "I was born to be a Fire Dog! There was never any doubt!"

Bells looked around at the other fire dogs and her heart swelled with pride. She was part of the team now. She had a very important job to do and she couldn't wait to get started.

But first, Bells and the rest of the fire dog team had to be fitted out with uniforms to wear whenever they were called out to work.

Bells wasn't sure about the brightly coloured harness. It felt tight and itchy, but Turnout assured her she would soon get used to it. "Your handler needs to be able to see you if it's dark or if you are working in a smoky room or building. And you see that?" Turnout nodded to a small box on the front of the harness. "That's a camera. It's a magic machine, that only humans know how to use. It shows your handler and the other fire crew where you are in a building even if they can't see you."

Bells looked down at the little box. How could the fire crew see her through such a tiny thing, she wondered. But she only wondered for a second because the itchy harness was driving her mad. She lay on the floor and rolled over a few times. Then she stood up and shook herself hard. The harness felt more comfortable now, and she thought that maybe Turnout was right – she would soon get used to it.

Then it was time to try on the special goggles or 'Doggles' that she would need to wear to protect her eyes from dust and debris in fire damaged and collapsed buildings, and the boots she would need to wear to protect her paws from broken glass and rubble.

Bells blinked a few times. The Doggles felt very odd and she was tempted to scrabble them off with her paws. But she knew Turnout would only growl at her if she did, so she sat quietly, twitching her nose from time to time as Poppy pulled the special boots over her paws.

"There!" said Poppy, standing back to inspect her. "Don't you look the part!"

Just then, a familiar voice called from across the room. "Bells! Bells! We're here, we're here!"

Bells turned her head and to her astonishment, there was Katie, Leah, and Dave rushing towards her. "I'm so sorry we're late," panted Katie. "The traffic coming into London was terrible, but we didn't want to miss this for the world!"

Katie gathered Bells in a warm, tight hug. "We've missed you so much," she said. "Poppy told us you'd passed all the tests. We knew you would! We had to come and see you get your special badge! You're a Fire Dog now, Bells. You're a Fire Dog!"

"Uff! Uff!" barked Bells happily. This was turning out to be the best day of her whole life. And to top it off, Katie, Leah and Dave stayed all evening and joined in the celebration party. There were sausages and cake crumbs galore, which Bells and the rest of the fire dog team wasted no time in gobbling up.

If this is what being a fire dog is all about, thought Bells, I want to be one forever!

18

It was late one night in the fire station when the signal first sounded. The crew was sitting around playing cards and Bells was lying under the table gnawing on a chew.

As the bell clanged loudly, and the shout of MOBILISE, MOBILISE, MOBILISE blared out of the fire station speakers, the fire crew jumped into action leaving their cards scattered across the table and their cups of tea to go cold.

Bells leaped up excitedly, her whole body on full alert and her chew forgotten. This was it! Her first job as a fire dog! With her tail whipping madly from side to side, Bells followed Poppy to where her harness was hanging and stood perfectly still while Poppy fastened it around her belly. Then she jumped into the fire engine and sat at Poppy's feet as the fire station doors opened and the engine roared out into the night.

As blue lights lit up the sky, Bells' heart was beating as loud and fast as the siren that was warning everyone to move out of the way. It wasn't long before the fire engine came to an abrupt stop. The doors were flung open and the fire crew began shouting instructions to one another. Bells' nose twitched. The smell of burning, smoke, and danger was everywhere.

She jumped out of the fire engine after Poppy and immediately felt the heat in the air. "Okay, girl, this is it," said Poppy as she strapped on Bells' doggles and boots. "It's time to go to work."

But Bells couldn't move. She wanted to. She wanted to fly into action and put all her training to use. But the sight of the burning house in front of her, the crackle and spit of the flames, and the stink of the thick, black smoke, left her rooted to the spot.

All she could think of was that terrible night when a fire as hot and fierce as this one took away her mother and brothers and sisters.

"Come on, girl," yelled Poppy. "We need to see if anybody's trapped inside!"

But still, Bells couldn't move. The fear she had felt on that night so long ago came rushing back. The scar behind her tail began to throb and before Poppy could stop her, Bells darted away from the fire and jumped back into the fire engine. She crawled under a seat and lay there trembling and wishing she was anywhere else but there.

"Bells! Bells! What's the matter, girl?" Poppy tried to coax her out. But Bells just buried her face in her paws and whined softly. In the distance, she could hear the shouts of the fire crew and the blast of water pumping from the hose. There was nothing Poppy could do or say to persuade Bells to come out from her hiding place – even her red ball couldn't tempt her.

The fire crew continued fighting the fire without her and eventually, Bells heard them all climbing back into the fire engine. Only when they arrived back at the station and everybody had gone their separate ways did Bells crawl out from under the seat.

Back at Poppy's house, once Poppy had gone upstairs to catch up on some sleep, Bells lay tossing and turning in her own bed. She couldn't stop thinking about what had happened. Why didn't she do her job? Why had she run to hide in the fire engine? She had let everyone down. She had let Poppy down. She had let the rest of the fire crew down. She had let Turnout down and most of all she had let herself down.

She thought again of the crackle and roar and heat of the fire and how it had made her feel like a frightened puppy again. She sighed deeply and slumped down in her bed. How could she ever do her job as a fire dog if she was so frightened of fire?

19

The morning dawned bright and breezy. Usually, Bells loved days like these, when her first walk was filled with the sound of birdsong and the wind rustling through the trees and ruffling her fur. The park was always busy with dogs and their humans and Bells could race around greeting everyone and catching up on the gossip.

But Bells wasn't in the mood today. She was too worried about what would happen when Poppy took her back to the fire station. What would Turnout say? He would be so angry and disappointed. Would he take away her badge and tell her she could no longer be a fire dog? She wouldn't be able to live with Poppy anymore and Katie wouldn't want her back either.

Where would she live? Who would want her? Then an awful thought came into Bells' mind. She remembered overhearing some dogs in the park talking about a place where unwanted dogs were sent. A place called a Dogs Home.

Dogs of every breed and age were sent to this place when their humans no longer wanted them. They were made to live in kennels of concrete with metal bars to stop them escaping. There was no sky in this place. Just endless grey walls and the yelps and howls of dozens of unloved dogs.

Bells shivered in horror. Was it possible that she was going to end up in a Dogs Home?

Later that morning, as Poppy and Bells arrived back at the fire station, Bells prepared herself to face Turnout. She felt sad down to her very bones at the way things had turned out. And if it was her fate to be sent to a Dogs

Home, then she only had herself to blame.

"Now then, Mutt," growled Turnout as he looked Bells up and down with his glittering eyes. "That was a pretty sorry display last night. What have you got to say for yourself?"

"I...I don't know," stammered Bells. "I just...I just saw that fire and I couldn't move. It was as if I was a puppy all over again, trapped in the burning shed with my mother and brothers and sisters."

"Mmmmm," murmured Turnout. "I thought as much. The Fear got to you, did it?"

Bells nodded. "Yes, and I'm sorry. I've let you down. I've let everyone down." She looked up at Turnout. "Will I have to go to a Dogs Home now?"

Turnout flashed his teeth. "A Dogs Home? Is that what you think?"

"But...but where else would I go, if I'm not a fire dog anymore?"

"Who said you're not a fire dog anymore?" asked Turnout.

"I...I thought because of last night, you wouldn't want me as part of your crew. What use is a fire dog who is afraid of fire?"

"That is a very good question, Mutt. A very good question. And I think the answer will surprise you." Turnout circled slowly around Bells, sniffing her coat and back legs and under her tail. Then he came face to face with her again and looked her straight in the eye.

"It is because you ARE afraid of fire that makes you a great fire dog. Your fear shows that you know how dangerous it is, how unpredictable it is, and how devastating it can be. Your fear shows how you respect fire. You may not believe it, but we are all afraid of fire. Even I am afraid of it. But we have learned how to turn our fear into bravery."

Bells' heart leaped. Was Turnout telling her it was okay to be afraid? That she could still be a fire dog?

"You have a great nose, Mutt," said Turnout. "One of the best. Next time the signal sounds and you are called out to a fire, just imagine you are on your way to rescue your mother and brothers and sisters. You can do this. I believe in you."

With that, Turnout padded off to his food bowl in the corner leaving Bells staring in wonder after him.

20

Turnout was right. As the weeks passed, Bells learned to turn her fear to good use. She knew that as soon as Poppy strapped the brightly coloured harness around her belly, it was time to work. If the harness was hanging on the wall then it was playtime, sleepy time and food time.

She learned to recognise all the bells and signals that rang out at the fire station and knew exactly which signal meant a fire was raging somewhere.

When the words MOBILISE, MOBILISE,

MOBILISE echoed around the fire station, Bells ran to where her harness was hanging and waited for Poppy to strap it on. Then she jumped in the fire engine and sat quiet and ready by Poppy's feet as the engine raced through the streets of London, its siren wailing and its blue lights flashing.

When Bells and her team arrived at the scene of a fire, Bells imagined her mother and family were trapped inside. If the building was clear, Bells waited behind the firefighters as they aimed the hoses. If the water ever splashed her way, Bells would nestle under one of the firefighters' coats.

When the fire had gone out and the building was cold, Bells would make her way inside dressed in her doggles and boots to sniff out and find what had caused the fire and where it had started. The only reward she ever needed was her treasured red ball.

Bells always sensed when a building wasn't clear, and she was always the first to leap off the fire engine and run into a burning building to scout for humans and animals in need of help. With the help of her doggy camera, the firefighters knew where to go to rescue the victims.

After a while, Bells had a new collection of scars and bruises from burns and broken glass and from falling off the fire engine when she jumped too quickly. But these new scars didn't make her sad like the old scar behind her tail did. These new scars were proof that she had rescued humans and animals and had won the fight against fire.

21

As the weeks and months passed and the weather turned warm, Bells often lay on the ground outside the fire station soaking up the sun. Turnout would sometimes join her and tell her hair-raising tales of the many rescues he'd been involved in. The one he spoke about most often was the terrible tower block fire that had killed hundreds of humans.

"I'll never forget it," he said. "Not to my dying day. I did my very best, but that fire was too fierce and monstrous for anyone to survive it." He sighed deeply, then turned to Bells and looked at her with watery eyes.

"I'm getting old now," he said. "It's almost time for me to retire. I'm looking forward to long, lazy days in my handler's garden and evenings curled up by the fire."

"But you can't retire," said Bells, her heart suddenly feeling too heavy for her chest. "You're the best. What would we do without you?"

"Ah, Mutt," said Turnout gently. "None of us can go on forever, no matter how brave we are. But you're wrong. I'm not the best anymore. You are. And I can retire in peace knowing that one day soon you will take my place as an instructor at the dog training school."

Bells lay her muzzle on her paws and blinked sadly. "You'll still come and visit us though, won't you?" she asked.

"Just try and stop me," chuckled Turnout. "Just try and stop me."

DAILY NEWS

Bells, a four-year veteran with the London Fire Brigade, made her eighth heroic rescue on the evening of September 2nd.

Although most of Bells' rescues to date have involved humans, on this particular evening she put a dog's disdain for cats to one side to do her duty. Using her well-honed skills to search every building for victims, Bells was able to save two kittens in desperate need of a hero.

On the evening in question, the London Fire Brigade responded to a report of a fire on the ground floor of a sweet shop in Paddington.

Upon their arrival, neighbours told the firemen that the building was empty, and that everyone had made it out safely. Bells ignored the humans. Trusting her nose, she made a dash for the burning building.

Singed and nearly overcome by smoke, she emerged from the building four minutes later with a kitten in her mouth. She laid the kitten at the feet of the Chief Firefighter, Les Jones.

She then gave a short warning bark and ran back into the building. Once again, she came back to the street carrying another kitten in her mouth. She refused medical attention until she had licked the kittens clean. Then she watched as a firefighter placed them inside a large, flannel-lined fireman's hat.

Once she knew the kittens were safe, Bells reported to the vet for treatment. After a few applications of burn salve, Bells was ready to go into action again. When the firemen returned to the fire station, they rewarded her with her favourite red ball and a large, marrow-filled bone.

The End

ABOUT THE AUTHORS

LES JONES got involved in firefighting in 1980 at 20 years old, and worked at a large chemical company. Due to its risk and hazards, the company had its own internal fire service. This continued into another chemical industrial role until 1996. He attended external training courses including attending the Fire Service College in Gloucestershire.

He became a member of the IFE (Institute of Fire Engineers) and sat their examination at Crewe Fire Station in 1994. He became assistant team leader of the eight-person crew on his shift and focused on training and fire drill events.

In 1996 he became a police officer and found himself torn between Policing and the Fire Service as he had opportunities with both organisations. He spent 20 years in both uniform and plain clothes duties.

STEVE EGGLESTON is a law school Vale-dictorian, former law professor, author, lecturer, and colourful trial lawyer. In his renaissance life, he has launched a hip-hop start-up, produced feature films, helmed a rock 'n roll magazine, booked 1000+ live shows worldwide, and managed Grammy-winning artists. As an international bestselling author, he is published in fiction and non-fiction and lives with his family in Somerset, England, where he draws and paints in his free time. Steve's business can be found on steveegglestonwrites.com.

ALSO BY LES JONES

Read about how Bells survived the fire that sadly killed her family in the novel *Twelve Doors,* available on Amazon.

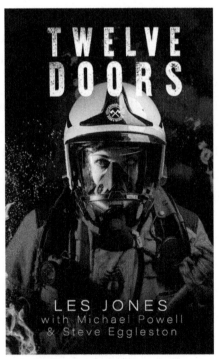

https://www.12doors.info